A Life Transformed: My Letter from Prison

By: Kimberly Phillips

I sit here today in the sunshine with my friend, trying to decide how to start this book. Which part of my life do I tell first? My actual birth? My rebirth in Christ Jesus? Or do I start somewhere in the middle with why I ended up in prison?

I was raised in the Church. The first time I gave my life to God, I was two years old and filled with the Holy Spirit at age four. Don't think that the Church is always perfect and protected. It's not. The enemy loves to sneak in to cause havoc, pain, fear, and every other destructive emotion and thought possible. From the age of five through age eight, I was sexually molested by family members. This was the enemy at work in the church and in my family's life. God says that anything the enemy means for destruction, He (God) will turn about for good. In my case, part of that good was coming to prison (Romans 8:28).

We are now in my valley of darkness

Pulling out my journals - all eleven of them - to walk that past in order to write all of this down. I want to and feel led by the Spirit to share my story so that your life can be impacted and healed by our Father, the Great "I Am." I am going to walk you hand in hand down and through my valley of darkness. Don't worry, God is with us in this journey of discovery and healing! (Joshua 1:5) Yes, God wept when the molestation occurred but I did not really start walking in that darkness until I chose to leave the church because of my family's falling apart. My father backslid and began drinking. I was about twelve years old, stopped going to church and began to hang out with boys and girls who chose worldly pursuits. We went to keggers, house parties, drinking and eventually adding drugs into the mix. I ran from God's calling on my life. I was fooled by the worldly strongholds, including drugs, fast living, and unhealthy relationships.

God has a theme going on here at the 7-Eleven

I won't say that I learned my lesson quickly like it's done in a two hour Hollywood movie. I ran for thirty years! Not even Sampson ran from God for that long. Do you remember the story of Jonah? He ran from the work God told him to do. His running was because he was afraid. Fear is a powerful motivator in our lives. How we allow that fear to be dealt with in our lives shows whether or not we trust God to take care of us in spite of the circumstances. That was my life at the time. I allowed my fears to rule me instead of trusting our Father to use that fear to refine and strengthen me. I became a female "Jonah."

Through all this running I had many encounters with both the enemy and God. Some of these negative encounters included: guns held to my head; beaten in a motel room that lasted days by a man whom I thought loved me; fell asleep at the wheel of my car and woke right before hitting a telephone pole; stayed up for seventeen days doing drugs while thinking that the Mexican Mafia was going to kill me; slept on stranger's back porches because I had nowhere else to go and many other such ugly encounters. God also created encounters for me to get my attention. One such encounter occurred while I was waiting in my boyfriend's car in the parking lot of a 7-Eleven. This couple was returning from a conference and were led by the Holy Spirit to stop at the 7-Eleven in order to give me a message. Now I did not know these people, had not ever met them before in my life. They asked if my name was Kimberly and I responded with "Who wants to know?" Let me remind you that God has a sense of humor because their response to my somewhat belligerent question was, "Jesus sent us here." I freaked out a bit and told them to back away from the car, "I'm not Kimberly." They said, "Yes you are." I asked how they knew this and they said they had come from a women's conference and the Holy Spirit told them my name, which car I was in, and to give me a message that the Lord is calling me back to Himself. I began to weep and said, "Please get away from the car before my boyfriend sees you." They walked away, got in their car and left. I still kept my Master on the shelf after that encounter. I was trying to deal with the drugs, the man, my kids, and not realizing that without God, I was nothing and had no hope of digging myself out of the quagmire I was in. You also need to keep in mind that I continued to keep a very tight hold on the pain I experienced as a five year old little girl. The abuse had me bound threefold: physically, mentally, and spiritually. I know this sounds confusing but be patient while I explain how tightly I was bound.

Physically, I was bound by my five year old self because of shame and guilt and wondering why God allowed the sexual abuse to happen to me. I know realistically I am not at fault but when you have been abused you don't think about laying the blame properly where it belongs. Mentally, I was bound by lies from the enemy, thinking, "I'd better not say anything because I wouldn't be believed." or "I was told not to say anything or something bad will happen to me." These chains are just as strong as the chains that held my physically. Now spiritually, my bondage kept me from crying out to God for help and release from the prison I put myself into. I felt unworthy of God's love, not mature enough to know the difference between healthy and unhealthy types of love. This also meant I felt unworthy of love. Period. Spiritually, I felt condemned, undervalued, unworthy, and was so broken in my spirit. I had scales on my eyes, watching my family fall apart, away from the church and from me.

I didn't know God so personally. That lack of attention from the church and my family also helped in creating my brokenness. These spiritual chains not only hurt the worst but were the hardest to break from. I know this is a really dark time in my valley but we have the light of God at our front and His armor covering us. (Ephesians 6:10) Just like God did for the man oppressed with legions of demons, casting them off of him and breaking those chains; God did the same for me. (John 5)

About two weeks after the first Godly encounter at the 7-Eleven, God provided another encounter at the same location! My boyfriend and I had an argument and he kicked me out of his car. The time was around 11:00 am, I was standing in the phone booth crying when a woman in a truck pulled up. She asked me if she could help me and give me a ride somewhere. I answered yes. When she came out of the 7-Eleven, we got in be truck and drove away from the store. I saw a picture of Jesus hanging from her rearview mirror and began to cry. She asked, "Did you know Jesus loves you and wants a relationship with you?" She then told me that I had put Him (God) on the shelf long enough. I knew in my heart she was right and for sure God was speaking through her. She then followed that up by saying, "I don't have a lot of money, but here's $20.00. God wants you to get something to eat and not spend it on drugs." She dropped me off at another 7-Eleven by a family member's house. I went in, bought a pack of cigarettes, a beer, and a .99 cent hamburger. I know, I think God has a theme going on here with the 7-Eleven convenience stores.

After this incident of being kicked out of the boyfriend's car and dropped off at another 7-Eleven by that wonderful woman of God, I was on a mission - a mission of survival. I think back to the story of David and how our stories are reminiscent of one another. We were not trying to survive through the situations in our lives. I felt like I was part of the social decay and the poor of the world. Do you think David felt like this while running from King Saul? Just like David felt lost - physically and emotionally - while running from King Saul. I also felt lost physically and emotionally. I lost all three of my children - the oldest to her father and the two younger to a woman of God who would take care of them and raise them in the ways of the Lord while keeping them safe. I also lost my family's trust, but they didn't know that I was keeping that destructive and devastating secret from my childhood. I lost my focus on who God said I was, my sense of self-worth; I lost everything, including my sense of reality. I shoved everything in order to hide from my five year old self and the abuse I suffered. How did I hide from this, you ask? Cocaine. Cocaine was my security blanket from the realities of life and my hiding spot from the pain and heartache I suffered due to the abuse. My soul was that bruised. It was bleeding from hiding and not dealing with the strains I suffered at 5 years old. I became addicted to gambling, alcohol, and the fast life. I didn't know how to survive in a Godly manner. Another similarity to David when he was king, he was addicted to adultery and polygamy. He had five wives and many other women on the side. Because he kept adding women to his marriage, God allowed the consequences of family turbulence. (2 Samuel 11: 1- 24; 25). The difference between David and me was the sins we committed and the type of relationship with God.

Unlike David, who had a deep intimate relationship with God, I did not. On top of the drugs and alcohol, I was a bartender, I lied, cheated, did anything and everything I could just to survive. I did not have the deep relationship with Christ that David had, nor did I have the proper tools to survive and thrive in a manner of which God would approve. I had the seed of Christ planted but was too adolescent to know how to water and feed that seed that had such potential for a deep abiding relationship with our Father. My punishment for my sins was the pain that I continued to go through while running away from reality, and the pain and suffering from my past that the enemy had me holding onto. I also chose to hold onto all that ugliness because it became a type of security blanket. Mind you, at the end of the day I blamed no one but myself for the prison in which I had made myself a captive. I allowed the men to keep abusing me and was blinded by my flesh and Satan to keep me there while forgetting that I had the basic tools to break out of that self-made prison - I had grown up in a God-fearing, Spirit-filled home. The deception I lived in from my various addictions, I believed I needed to stay in that self-made prison with the feeling of despair and hopelessness that I would be nothing more than an alcoholic, a drug addict, a gambler. Nowhere did I see any chance of change in what I saw as my identity. Fortunately, God had and still has a broader aspect of my identity. He did say He knows the plans He has for me in Jeremiah 29:11. Of course, He also said that He knows the amount of hair on my head and the number of tears that I cry, He collects those tears as precious jewels. (Psalms 56:8; Matthew 10:30)

Brave Enough?

My friend Hollie, who is working with me on this book, has a book by Cheryl Strayed titled *Brave Enough.* (2015) It has some amazing quotes that really relate to my life and may even relate to yours. One of these quotes relates to my alcoholism and cheating. Strayed says, "Most people don't cheat because they're cheaters. They cheat because they're people. They are driven by hunger or for the experience of someone being hungry once more for them. They find themselves in friendships that take an unintended turn or they seek them out because they're horny or drunk or damaged from all the stuff they didn't get when they were kids. There is love. There is lust. There is opportunity. There is alcohol. And youth. And middle age. There is loneliness and boredom and sorrow and weakness and self-destruction and idiocy and arrogance and romance and ego and nostalgia and power and need. There is the compelling temptation of intimacies with which one is most intimate. Which is a complicated way of saying it's a long...life. And people get mucked up in it from time to time. Even the people we marry. Even us." (107)

How true is that quote in all our lives! I bet it was true during David's life as well. After the last encounter with God, I continued to walk in all my more and muck - meaning God was still on the shelf.

In another quote, Strayed asks the question, "How did you get your water?"(95) Obviously I wasn't getting my water from our Father. There was no living water flowing in my life to continue watering those seeds that God had planted. I was totally restricted by the enemy's plans and not Gods. I hated the place that I was stuck in. The negative thoughts would not stop swirling in my head and as I thought I was having a good time in this destructive behavior, I was in fact living aimlessly, getting arrested again and again for stupid traffic violations. This behavior pattern soon had me performing a higher level of crime. I was lying to men to get money. They wanted relationships so I sold myself to them. It was a form of prostitution. I sold them a dream to support everything I had become addicted to and was feeling betrayed by my past and the abuse that I went through. I took it out by not giving them sex but reaping the ill gotten benefits by making them think that by giving me what I wanted, they might eventually get what they wanted. I would get them to take me to their banks and withdraw very large sums of money while having them think that pleasing me was their biggest goal and life achievement and maybe even a future with me. Of course some of them just wanted to satisfy their perverted desires. Thinking that I was getting away with this and avoiding what had happened to me, I continued to manipulate and cheat men out of their money to try to make myself feel whole. Not targeting any particular man, just those that wanted to treat me like the men treated me in the past, a sex abuse victim. This added to those chains that I spoke on earlier. I feel that this part of my life was going to impact the lives of others some day and maybe not in a positive way, including mine. Knowing at the time it was a quick fix to covering up my suffering and my addictions that my suffering caused.

Psalms 32:5 says,

> I acknowledged my sin to you,
> and I did not cover my iniquity;
> I said, "I will confess my transgressions to
> the LORD," and you forgave the
> iniquity of my sin.(ESV)

1 Peter 4:8 says,

> Above all, keep loving one another earnestly,
> since love covers a multitude of sins. (ESV)

I obviously did not follow these two scriptures. How could I when I could not acknowledge even to myself, let alone the Lord, what my sins were and did not know how to love others, let alone myself. I was still running like David and Jonah. I knew that I was going to be swallowed up soon by some type of whale. God has an interesting way of really, truly getting our attention and stopping us from running. He knew and heard in my spirit my cry to Him but I was not strong or brave enough to ask for help.

Strayed says about bravery, "Bravery is acknowledging your fear and doing it anyway." (106) I was drawn to what was evil that kept me trapped in continuing my wicked deeds and being one of those who was an evildoer. Being a part of eating from the Babylonian's delicacies, I didn't know what was going to manifest through all this darkness in which I was trapped. I knew someday that I would fall into my own net that I had created. This net was the decayed seed that I kept feeding and watering through my negative behavior and actions. I was lost and broken and taking it out on everyone that came into my path.

God's plan would not fail

WOW, let's review this together! Born into a faith based home, sexually abused at five, started drinking and smoking cigarettes at nine and one thing led to another. I started smoking weed, then dropped out of school in the sixth grade. Wow, can you believe it? The six grade. WOW, I am now fifty-one years old and looking back on everything that the Lord has brought me through. His plan would not fail. What I hadn't realized was that God had been waiting for this moment all my life with incredible love and patience. He bore through my years of sin, eager for this moment when He would cause me to love Him as deeply as He loved me. I realized He was weeping through all this darkness. I didn't know when enough was going to be enough. I just knew that I was getting close to my rock bottom. And we all know that once you hit bottom, there is nowhere to go but up. I also realized that the prison that I kept myself in was going to be used for my benefit and God's glory. Remember Jeremiah 29:11 - Evil will be turned for our benefit and God's glory. We need to remember that even through our valleys, God is not only with us but is also working and arranging things for our benefit; things that will make us better people and stronger in our loving Lord. Though I couldn't see how at that moment, God would definitely show me over time. Little did I know then that I was on my way to experiencing things I would never dream could happen - to me and for me. This is where the seed of healing begins to grow.

Strayed said, "That place of true healing is a fierce place. It's a giant place. It's a place of monstrous beauty and endless dark and glimmering light. And you have to work really, really, really hard to get there, but you can do it." (56) As we continue to walk through my valley and begin to see the other side, you will see how hard I had to work to reach my healing. I then began to go to my older sister Debbie's house, telling her I could no longer live this path of self-destruction. You ask how I came to this decision? I was going to die either by the man that I was living with - he was very abusive - or I was going to go to prison for the crimes that I believed I had to do to survive. I know that Gods says in Isaiah 5:13a,

Therefore my people go into exile
for lack of knowledge. (ESV)

Mind you, not only was I at my sister's house telling her this, I was still continuing the self-destructive behavior of drinking, drugs and gambling. I knew that my second prison term was going to manifest sooner rather than later. At the age of nineteen, I had done three and a half years in prison for the same behavior that I would eventually serve in prison for again.

Taken into captivity

Captivity is a curse and can become a generational curse. How did I end up in prison for the second time in my life? This is easy to answer. I broke the law and was arrested. I went to jail. However, where does God fit in with all of this? Deuteronomy 28: 64-67 states,

> "Then the Lord will scatter you [take thou into captivity] among all nations...Among those nations you will find no repose, no resting place for the sole of your foot. There the Lord will give you an anxious mind, eyes weary with longing, and a despairing heart. You will live in constant suspense, filled with dread both night and day, never sure of your life. In the morning you will say, "If only it were evening!" and in the evening, "If only it were morning!" - because of the terror that will fill your hearts and the sights that your eyes will see." (author's emphasis).

Why would God take me into captivity? For one thing, I broke fellowship with him and refused to listen each time He sent someone to me to tell me to come back to Him. Remember the 7-Eleven experiences? The bible also says, "long ago, even before He made the world, God chose us to be His very own." (Ephesians 1:4) This scripture should give you a better idea why God hated my life on streets. My actions created separation from God. The Bible is filled with real life people whose actions also separated them from God. To heal this relationship, God took me into captivity, cleansed me of my sin and restoring me back to Him. This sounds really easy and simple but it wasn't. I had to work at it.

Another reason why God will take me into captivity is because He has a purpose for my life other than the one I had been pursuing. God did not create me to live the life I was choosing to live. I needed help with the pain I was carrying around. I was chasing after the healing that only God could perform. I left my sister's house and began aimlessly treading the streets again, not knowing my second prison term was right around the corner.

With the idea of prison right around the corner I want to tell you all the destructive behaviors that God had already brought me through was a complete miracle after miracle after miracle. You already know about the alcohol and gambling and the manipulation of me to gain money, what you are going to learn further about me may resonate with your life. You know the root of these behaviors - me being molested at five years of age – and because of this, at nine, I was going to, and participating in, keggers; at ten, I was smoking weed; at thirteen, I was smoking weed and cigarettes; and at the age of sixteen, I was using cocaine and acid. I became pregnant at seventeen with my oldest daughter Katrina Marie Phillips. After birthing her, I lived with her father who introduced me to "wet" - a derivative of angel dust. My use of crack cocaine increased massively at this time also. I had been so stressed out, I left Katrina's dad and took Katrina with me . . . everywhere, including crack houses. I finally got so tired of my daughter watching me while not understanding what was going on, I let her father start to keep her more often.

Then it just so happened that one day in my darkest hour that I was in the crack house sleeping that the doorbell rang. I got up and answered the door and a clean looking man was standing there and asked me "Are you Kimberly Phillips?" I said yes and asked why. He said he had some paperwork for me to sign from Richard Thayer - a restraining order against me from CPS Child Protection Agency in regards to my baby girl Katrina. I was willing to sign but very devastated. I was feeling like Jonah in the belly of the whale. I had nowhere to run and was stuck until God decided to let my whale spit me out. This, I soon found out, was only the whale's mouth. I later found out that the belly was my second stint in prison. I seemed to have it all together outwardly, but inside I was a wreck. I was so numb, broken, crushed, and wounded that I sat and cried because my baby girl was being taken away from me. I also had a sense of relief knowing she was out of harm's way because of my self-destructive behavior. Then I had the excuse to continue to stay in the self-destructive lifestyle. When was it all going to end? It didn't end with my first stint in prison where I not only did forty-three months but also had my third child while inside these gates. Obviously I continued that same behavior that landed me in prison the first time because I ended up serving a second sentence. Before coming to prison the first time, I lost my parental rights and full custody of my oldest daughter and gave birth to my second daughter, loosing custody of her as well. I started my first stint in prison in 1989. While serving my first sentence, I gave birth to my son Kurtis and lost custody of him. Being that I came to prison a second time, I apparently did not learn the lesson that God wanted me to learn the first time around. Jonah had a similar experience. My bible gives a commentary on Jonah. It says that Jonah "was a reluctant prophet given a mission he found distasteful. He chose to run away from God rather an obey Him. Sometimes we find ourselves wanting to turn and run. But it is better to obey God than to defy Him or run away. Often, in spite of our defiance, God in his mercy will give us another chance to serve him when we return to him." This is so true for all our lives. We have a tendency to allow fear of the unknown to rule us instead of the Great I AM. When this happens, you will notice that life tends to get rougher for you. You can see it did in my life when I ran from God. It got rougher for Jonah too when he ran from God. This running is why I had two stints in prison - the second where I finally relented and repented for my defiance and rededicating my life to Him and His will.

Planted in the soil of forgiveness, freed from emotional bondage

For my second stint in prison, I was sentenced to twenty-eight years, seven months for theft and swallowed up in my own belly of the whale. I was so at peace with it all being over. This is where Jesus really got my attention and I finally submitted to His will for my life. I just wanted to be in love with Jesus and be healed and repent of all I had done to many innocent people - the families that I hurt, my family, my kids, and the communities that I left wondering why I would take them for granted?

I needed help and this whale God had ordained from the very thought of my existence, just like Jonah, after my sentencing that really shook my family and kids to the core. I knew that I needed God's presence to direct me in every step I was going to take after this. I was afraid but I had a sense of who the master really was. But I was still a baby in many ways so this journey was going to be my last chance to really see what God 's purpose was in my life for his glory. Joyce Meyer's book *Beauty for Ashes* (2003) has a section that really correlates with my walk. Under the heading, "Do You Want To Be Free and Well?" it states,

> "Gaining freedom from emotional bondage is not easy.
> I will be honest from the beginning and say, point blank,
> that for many, many people reading this book, it will not
> be easy. It will provoke feelings and emotions they
> have been "stuffing" rather than facing and dealing
> with. You may be one of those people. You may have
> experienced feelings and emotions in the past that have
> been too painful to deal with, so each time you have
> come to the surface you have said to God,
> 'I'm not ready yet, Lord! I'll face at problem later!'

Meyer's book deals not only with the emotional pain caused by what others may have done to you, but also with your responsibility to God for overcoming those traumas and getting well. As Meyers says, "some people (actually a great number of people) have a hard time accepting personal responsibility." In a very practical way, Meyer's writes about dealing with "forgiveness, repressed anger, self-pity, the chip-on-the-shoulder syndrome, the you-owe-me attitude and many, many other poisonous mental and emotional attitudes that will need cleansing if you are ever to be fully well." You may be asking, Meyer writes,

> "But, who will deal with the person who hurt me? You may also be wondering, 'What makes this woman think that she is such an authority on the subject of emotions - especially mine?' You may have questions you would like to ask me, such as: 'Do you have a degree in psychology? Where did you do your study? Have you been through any of the things I am going through? How do you know what it is like to be caught in an emotional prison?'"

Meyer answers to all those questions and then adds, "and if you are brave enough to face your situation and have determined that you really want to get well, then read on." (10-11).

With what you have read so far of my journey through my valley of darkness, you can see how much the truth of these statements from Joyce Meyer resonated with me. I wanted to get truly well but it took a second term in prison to finally be "brave enough" to face my issues.

I have been in county jail many times for traffic violations and other petty crimes. However, the last time I was in county jail, I had turned myself in. I had hit rock bottom and wanted to stop hurting people. I wanted to start the journey of being held accountable for the way I treated others and was sick and tired of the way I treated others because of my personal demons. It was time for a positive change in my life but I wasn't going to be able to do it by myself. I needed God for sure and was finally admitting that I needed His assistance to clean up the mess I made of my life. I needed to be uprooted from the bad soil and transplanted in the soil of Jesus Christ - soil that will feed the seeds He planted in me including love, compassion, mercy, and forgiveness. This would get me out of the rut I was in because of the years of abuse and rejection I had gone through. All I could think was to get all of this - the affects of abuse from others and from myself to myself - behind me.

Lorenzo, my abusive boyfriend at the time, and I drove up to Pierce county Washington from Oregon going 80 mph the whole way. During the drive, Lorenzo kept begging me not to turn myself in, especially since I was on Washington's most wanted at the time. He didn't understand that I was tired of the life I was living, including the physical abuse I received from him.

I was bound and determined to turn myself in to the cops before Lorenzo killed me. I also called my brother and sister in-law to ask them to go with me to turn myself in. I told them that I wanted to be accountable and take responsibility for my actions. They said that they would be waiting for me and that this was the best decision I could make for my life. I met them by Spanaway Lake in Spanaway where my brother was doing a cleaning and roofing job. When I got there I said I'm ready to go. I handed his wife my leather coat, purse, and cigarettes then got in his car. He shut down the house he was working on and then called the Pierce County Jail to let them know that they were bringing me in and that I was on Washington's Most Wanted. Mind you, Lorenzo was following the entire way blaring his horn to get me to stop and not turn myself in.

We arrived and the police said that there was not a warrant for me so they would not book me. We told them that they made a mistake, but I was not leaving until they found my warrant. It took them 45 minutes before they found the warrant and I was handcuffed. I then cried for six months strait while God was cleansing my body of all the drugs, including the cocaine that I had put in my body. For the next year I focused on reestablishing my relationship with Christ, learning all I could about him and going to every bible study and church service I could. I finally began seeking Jesus more than anytime previously in my life. I shared all I knew with anyone who would listen and pursued a personal relationship with Jesus Christ.

As I waited for the charges that were being brought against me, I was still in denial. I was still lying to myself about what had happened to me and did not know how to tell the truth of this after hiding it for so long. I knew I had hurt a lot of people in my life but didn't know how God was going to turn it around. Trusting God is hard, especially when you can't see the light at the end of the tunnel and nothing but darkness surrounds you.

Behold, I will do a new thing

I spent twelve and a half months in county jail dealing with myself and working on changes that God needed me to make in order to become the woman of God that He wants me to be.

Let me tell you about this time in jail. It is another section of my valley but getting closer to the other end. For the first time in my life I was ready to deal with my past and allow God to heal me from my past. The inner woman in me needed the new beginning that God promises us in Isaiah 43:18-19. This verse states,

> Remember not the former things,
> nor consider the things of old.
> Behold, I am doing a new thing;
> now it springs forth, do you not perceive it?
> I will make a way in the wilderness
> and rivers in the desert. (ESV)

The Baker Commentary on this verse states, "This new thing refers to the new era of forgiveness, restoration, and God's presence. The servant of Yahweh, the people whom he has chosen, will be refreshed", which was exactly what I was looking for in my search for God. I know that the commentary also speaks true when it says, "[His] rivers of water speak not only of the spiritual refreshment but also about the manner in which Yahweh will take care of the physical needs of his people in bringing them out of exile and into the Promised Land.

The very purpose of the deliverance is that the people praise Yahweh upon experiencing the blessings of redemption and restoration." I knew of this promise but the process would mean God would have to bring me through a total transformation. We all know that transformation often deals with some form of pain. As I sat in Pierce county jail waiting for either a plea bargain or trial, I read my Bible literally twelve hours a day over and over and over. During this time God's word began revealing the secret places that I was running from. This is where the pain comes in, dealing with those issues that you would rather pretend didn't exist. I was trying to deal with all this emotional trauma that not only was dealt to me but also what I dealt out to others. There is no way I could do this on my own, hence, the crying out to God and reading His word like it was my only lifeline, because it was.

Believe it or not, the addictions were gone! I was done. I craved nothing but God and my new lease on life serving Him. I was praying about the choices brought to me - to take the plea bargain of ten years or go to trial. My family and Lorenzo told me to take it to trial. I didn't know how to hear God's still small voice so I didn't know what the right choice would be. I chose trial that turned out to be the wrong choice - Satan won another point on that one. I didn't know better as I was relearning how to listen and follow God. I was a baby all over again. But to go back a bit and tell of some of the experiences I had while in county jail... I was sent a Catholic chaplain who called me out and said that God sent him with a message to tell the truth and there would be a blessing in telling the truth. I had difficulty in doing this because of that nasty little thing called fear. I was still in denial and needed God to make some changes within me so that I could obey him.

I began attending every service and came to be really close to the volunteers. Through this I re-received the baptism of the Holy Spirit - my personal prayer language of speaking in tongues. Acts 2 speaks of prayer in tongues and the baptism of the Holy Spirit. I had originally received my prayer language as a small child as I had mentioned earlier in this book.

Mind you, praying in my secret language that only God can understand started cleansing me of my past, healing me and causing that transformation that I so badly needed God to do. Drinking of the cup of God ignited the spiritual warfare in breaking those heavy, heavy chains I had wrapped around myself in my former life. Then.... some new visitors came to see me. They brought me the same message that the Catholic chaplain had brought me. I didn't know how to tell the truth but so badly wanted to comply with God. I was so adolescent and immature in God that I kept finagling others to attempt to be spared some of the time I was facing.

As my court proceedings kept being put off, I received visits from my family and Lorenzo. They kept repeating over and over "Do not take the deal, do not take the deal." I was so confused as to what the right decision was to make. As I continued to read the Word and pray, I felt my trial looming right around the corner. Now remember, I also had to keep in mind the message that God kept sending me - tell the truth. Telling the truth is such a scary thing sometimes. Ask Paul. He lied, cheated, and murdered until God set him right in a very drastic way. He literally knocked him off of his mule and blinded him for an extended period of time.

Mind you, I was not grown up enough nor had I worked on myself enough to do as God bid. I know I needed to tell the truth but I was so scared. It has taken me twenty-five years to create the old me - an addict and manipulator. Because of my fear, and shame of my past, I wasn't sure what God was going to do and how much time I was going to be facing but I truly wanted to be accountable and finally get the help I needed and be honest to all the people I had hurt. So God made sure that man gave me a prison sentence that would get my attention. I was asked to take the deal of a ten year sentence two more times but said no each time. I went to trial instead. I had no family there for my trial. No support. I drug each and every person I had injured in some way to testify. I neglected my kids while doing this behavior.

Standing in that courtroom, I was at rock bottom. I can't imagine what Joseph felt like when he went before Potiphar and then Pharaoh (Genesis 39:20-23; 41: 14-36) or how Saul –
renamed Paul - felt when he was thrown in prison then sent to Caesarea to face King Agrippa for judgment (Acts 25:13-27).

The difference in our guilt was my guilt was for hurting others while their guilt was for following the Lord. On my last day of trial I told God that no matter what happened I would surrender to His will. I needed Him to show me what His will was for me. The jury went into deliberation and I went back to my cell. No sooner had I gotten to my room, I was called back to the courtroom to hear the decision. They said I was guilty of all charges. That was the truth. As I sat there weeping, I was brought back to my cell for the second time. I got on my bed and began praying, telling God that I trusted Him even though I didn't know how to trust Him.

Believe it or not I was at peace. It felt like this enormous weight had been removed from my shoulders. I was finally being held accountable for my actions and taking responsibility.

On December 5, 2008, I went to my sentencing hearing. The courtroom was packed with my family, pastors, and friends on one side and the victim's families were on the other. The judge was asking if anyone in the courtroom if there was anyone who would like to speak on my behalf. My sister and brother both spoke for me and there were a few people who spoke upon the victim's behalf. The judge then proceeded to ask me if there was anything I wanted to say before he sentenced me. I said, "Yes sir." I got up and faced everyone in the courtroom and told everyone that I was wrong and apologized to them. There were many in the courtroom who were crying, including me. I proceeded to sit down and the Judge started talking, telling me that what I had done was wrong. Thinking at the time that no matter whatever amount of time was given, God was in control. He then told me to stand and sentenced me with eight counts of 1st degree theft for 343 months. That equals twenty-eight years and seven months. This time frame is considered an exceptional sentence and goes beyond the high end of the sentencing guidelines.

Now remember, God knows what He is doing. He knew what he was doing when Joseph was thrown in jail and he knew what he was doing when the judge sentenced me. I was crying so hard because of the exceptional sentence. It felt like everything just piled atop me. All I could do was cry out to God to help me. Everyone in the courtroom was crying now, even the cameraman for King5 News. I signed the papers and was dismissed from the courtroom. It still hadn't hit me and as I was waiting for the other two offenders have their turn before the judge, I held my head down and cried. I was crying so hard and loud that the Judge had to tell me to quiet down. Court proceeded and the other two were sentenced. They brought me back to my room. I was then called out by one of the senior officers in the pod who asked me if I needed a hug. I replied that I did and promptly started crying like a baby. She told me that everything was going to be all right and the time they gave me was totally ridiculous. As I proceeded to my bed after speaking with her, another officer who was a former professor, knelt down by my bed and told me told me that she had seen me on TV and that God had a plan. She was also weeping and told me that was totally unfair with what they had given me but to be all that I can be while in prison.

A vision from God

Between my sentencing and leaving for prison I had three unexpected visitors. The chaplain that I had spoken of before came and told me again that God was going to do exceedingly and abundantly above what I could think. Another chaplain came and told me that she had a vision that God had pulled me out of a little hole from the prison and there was many people following, wanting to surrender themselves to Christ. Then the next day a Filipino couple came to see me. They were volunteers with a ministry for the Pierce County Jail. They asked if they could speak with me and had me brought to a room where we had bible study. The husband told me that God sent them to tell me that I would not do all the time the judge gave me and don't ask when, how, and why. Only God knew the plans He had for me as it states in Jeremiah 29:11. They prayed over me and said for me to surrender to God's will. I haven't seen them since that day but kept that prophesy in my heart. On December 10, 2008, I was transferred to Washington Correction Center for Women (WCCW). I wanted the world to know how sorry I was and truly still am - it hurts me every breath I take I know that my life is truly changed but my heart is still so sorry.

Chains broken, yokes removed – transformation from the inside out

Well let's move on - I just had a moment - please bare with me. I am determined to do and be all I can be on this journey, so that my life can glorify God. I wanted to be able to make up for the innocent lives I had hurt. I felt that I owed them such a transformation from the ugly person that I had been. I began to work on myself in every way that I could - church services, obtaining my GED, working, self-help classes, praying, Kiros four-day retreat. These things allowed God to bring a lot of truths to light, chains broken, and yolks removed, especially during the Kiros retreat. This special event was so transformational because of His presence. This feeling is what I had been thirsting for during the entire time I held myself in the prison of my past, wanting to be accountable and searching for that elusive something in that my life so desperately needed. I knew that my transformation would be a long process but this type of work on myself would renew my mind to be set free from old behaviors and old ways of thinking. I wanted to forgive everyone that had hurt me in my past along with those I had hurt. I knew that these types of classes would help that process along. At this stage in my process of my life transformation I wanted the community to see that transformation from the inside out, not just a certificate on paper that I completed something. I needed them to see a "new" me, someone so changed by God that they would not recognize me upon first seeing me. I needed to do this for myself as well as my family and friends to give them hope that people can change and be transformed and redeemed and rehabilitated by our great and mighty Lord God.

I began working tirelessly, honoring my vow to God, encouraging everyone in the prison . . . staff included. I received visits from my parents three times a week for the first five years of my sentence, praying with them and telling them the amazing things that God was doing in my life from healings to restorations.

I spent only two weeks in CCU (Closed Custody Unit) before God had me transitioning to MSU (Medium Custody Unit). I began working in the kitchen shortly after moving down to MSU. It was my first job. Working in the kitchen is a very humbling experience. My first position was sanitization and washing pots and pans. One day I did one position and the next the other. I began serving the women as God led me to be a servant to them under all circumstances. It was very difficult. Imagine what David had to go through in learning how to be not only a leader to God's people but also a servant to them so that they could see the love of God, their Creator. This was a similar situation for me so that the women here at WCCW could see God's love and forgiveness for them. He also kept telling me that there was a future and a hope for the women here. He then began ministering to me and using me to minister to the women, like Ezekiel 37 states. Just like God showed Ezekiel how to bring life to dry bones by prophesying to them the word of the Lord, He taught me the same; to speak and prophesy to the dry places in the women's lives here (37:4-14). He was showing me that He had ordained me from my mother's womb to speak God's word to the dry places in the women's lives, bringing them the only water that can restore them, living water.

I began growing and transforming as God continued to work in and through me. There were signs and wonders, miracles in many of the women's lives. God had this all planned for His glory and many souls were saved as women received Him as their personal allowing His presence to soak into my being and work on healing me. I did this for two years straight. With the help of the Holy Spirit through volunteers at leadership services, the power of prayer had destroyed the yolk on my neck. As Isaiah 10:27 states,

> And in that day his burden will depart from your
> shoulder, and his yoke from your neck; and the yoke
> will be broken because of the fat." (ESV)

This is what happened to me because I could feel God's presence as he worked me through this process. You wonder how I could tell? I became more confident because of His strength and began forgiving myself for my past. I wanted to be able to tell the truth so that I could be truthful in God's ministry.

God expanded my territory

I signed up for every church service that I could possibly get into. God started transitioning me from working in the kitchen to working in the unit as a janitor. I was still being a servant to the women but in a different capacity. It wasn't easy to clean up after the women in the bathrooms and day room. God was humbling me even more. I was cleaning up after 150 women. Also I was praying the Jabez prayer, asking God to expand my territory (1 Chronicles 4: 10).

> Jabez called upon the God of Israel, saying, "Oh
> that you would bless me and enlarge my border,
> and that your hand might be with me, and that you
> would keep me from harm so that it might not
> bring me pain!" And God granted what he asked. (ESV)

I didn't really know what I was asking for but apparently God felt I was ready because He sure did expand my territory! As I continued in this new ministry of ministering and cleaning after women, I was also going to the house of God to be continuously filled to overflowing with the Spirit of the

Lord so that my cup could overflow onto the other women here (Psalms 23: 5).

> You prepare a table before me
> in the presence of my enemies;
> you anoint my head with oil;
> my cup overflows. (ESV)

My change in attitude caused a ripple effect

I started forming really close relationships with some of the women here that God put into my path. Some of them became family such as Maribel Gomez, Hollie Beston, and Donna Whisenhunt who was a disabled woman that I cared for until her death. There was also legitimate family here in the prison with me like Natalie Ray who is family through marriage. I also had two nieces here: Allie and her sister Valerie Horton. These relationships were used to strengthen me and my family. He even brought in people who knew me on the streets and were deeply affected by how much God has changed me. My change in attitude caused a ripple effect that changed other's perspective of me and of prison to a more forgiving and restorative idealism.

At this time in my life, seeing God's transformation on my life, I finally felt free of my past and gave the women in here hope that they can be free too. Freedom isn't just a physical action, it is also a state of being. I was finally free both spiritually and mentally. Of course, the facility only provided a very limited list of rehabilitative programming because of my length of sentencing. This basically consisted of church and more church. That is what God used to transform me. I eventually transferred to work in the chapel library where God used the gifts He gave me to lay hands on His daughters and pray for them just like Isaiah 61 says,

> The Spirit of the Lord GOD is upon me,
> because the LORD has anointed me

> to bring good news to the poor;
> he has sent me to bind up the brokenhearted,
> to proclaim liberty to the captives,
> and the opening of the prison to those who are bound. (ESV)

I was seeing this verse manifest right in front of me as I continued to do His will. I know that God was being glorified through this process. That was all that mattered to me now because in the past I would put Him last. Now I was making sure that He came first with the deeds that I did and any decision I needed to make. This included talking to Him first before acting or talking - at least most of the time. No one is perfect and we are all learning as God is working on us. As God worked it to keep me in the chapel for four years, I learned a lot about the heart of God and the duplicity of the enemy.

God kept me on the potters wheel and allowed me to be afflicted so that I would be made into a beautiful and colorful gem just like his word promises us in Isaiah 54:11.

> O afflicted one, storm-tossed and not comforted,
> behold, I will set your stones in antimony,
> and lay your foundations with sapphires. (ESV)

This is an incredible promise from the Word of God. As my journey went on I really pressed in and was so hard on myself. Never once did I get lazy. I was truly allowing the process to heal me from my rock bottom and renew my heart and mind. It changed and transformed my character as well. I prayed and prayed for the lives I had hurt and began to forgive myself and hope someday God would manifest their forgiveness. I worked on myself and did exactly what I was supposed to do to become a transformed person. I owed this to the victims and their families as well as myself, my family, my kids, grandkids and the community. I pressed on and knew that if I was who I proclaimed to be, it would manifest in my actions.

I then was asked to work in the offices of the big wigs—lieutenant, sergeant, social superintendant, captain, and other officers—basically, a high-risk area! I was in prayer for sure asking God if this was a door He wanted me to walk through? Sure enough, I was given confirmation through prayer and transferred into the job. I knew that this was truly new territory that God was leading me into and I needed to stay focused on this responsibility. I knew this assignment was for God's Glory to be revealed. I got together with one of my best friends and main prayer partner, Hollie, as often as our schedules would allow. We began praying for the women here, our families, the staff, individual needs – ours, and others. We always asked what God's will was for each prayer.

I knew that this new job would be a test of trust as I continuously found personal jewelry, cell phones, keys, etc. I also had to keep a lock on my tongue as I often heard information that was not to be passed beyond that building. The manifestation of the fruit of that labor of trust and prayer was me being asked to come back for another eighteen month term.

One thing I will share is that I heard about many victories that God had done in the staff's lives. I kept my job and the professional relationships—which I developed while in this position—in constant prayer. After another ten months, I was moved back to the chapel to work again. Remember God has been orchestrating my every move. I did not know that I would be sent to Yakima County Jail for seven days, but God did. Administration from WCCW called the jail and told them to bring me back. God said that seven days was enough for me and the assignment He had for me was completed. It had been a miracle God showed me that He truly orders our footsteps.

Jeremiah 33:3 states that if we call upon the Lord, He will show us great and mighty things. This is something that Hollie and I have been praying for the last two or three years. God started showing us things that would occur in our own lives and in the lives of many of the women for which we have been praying. That trip to Yakima was proof of this verse because according to WCCW, I should have stayed for six months, but God said seven days. Numbers are important to our Father. They have meaning. As I went back through the moving cycle from receiving to CCU, I noticed that my feeling seemed bleak. You know that feeling where life seems dark and everything that occurs to you negatively seems unfair. However, I continued to put my trust in the Lord, knowing He had something planned. Joel Osteen says in his book, *Blessed in the Darkness, How all things work for your good* that,

> "There are times in all our lives when things
> are not changing as fast as we would like...
> It's a night season. In these night seasons,
> we can't see what God is doing. It doesn't
> look as though anything is happening, but
> God is working behind the scenes. He does
> His greatest work in the dark...God hasn't
> forgotten about us. In the dark times,
> when life feels unfair, you have to remind
> yourself that God is still in control.
> Just because you don't see anything happening
> doesn't mean that God is not working...you
> have to learn to trust Him in the night
> seasons when things aren't going your way and
> you don't see anything happening. The night
> seasons are times of testing, times of proving." (pg 19-20)

This is where I was when I entered CCU upon returning from Yakima. I knew that God was doing something in me during this "night season" He was using the darkness around me to keep my metamorphosis. Osteen says that

"...God uses the dark places. They're a part of His divine plan. Think of a seed. As long as a seed remains in the light, it cannot germinate and will never become what it was created to be. The seed must be planted in soil, in a dark place, so that the potential on the inside will come to life. In the same way, there are seeds of greatness in us - dreams, goals, talents, potential - that will only come to life in a dark place." (pg 2)

This is where I am at now as Hollie and I write this book. God is germinating new seeds within me as He prepares me for my physical freedom from prison and my valley of darkness that we have been walking through in this book.

Remember, I have not given up on you

Don't think that I have given up on you for I have not, says the Lord and the hand that I put on you years ago is still upon you and I will make it more evident in the days to come...I send this word as a reminder to you that I have not forgotten what I have said over you though you may count years and days. The Lord says I do not count as men count. The Lord says... I walk you thru the dry places so you will appreciate the fertile places...I walk you through the hard places grow you in areas of strength but the Lord says across the nations of the world I am about to move in a new way...I am about to cause the places that were dry to become fertile and the hearts that were hard to become soften. You say it is impossible and I keep saying quit agreeing with the enemy and believe the voice of the Lord. In the last days says the Lord, I will pour out my Spirit upon all flesh your sons and daughters will prophesy. I have not changed my mind, I will pour out my Spirit on your offspring, I will pour out my glory on your children and your children's children and I will keep every word I have said to you...let every man be a liar but the word of God be true...therefore rejoice says the Lord and be glad and worship me for what I am about to do in the nations, and for what I am about to change in your life, for what I am about to restore to you. I am the God of abundance and I am the God of plenty so take off your mourning and spirit of heaviness, and put on the garment of praise and I will restore everything that has been stolen from you says the Lord. This word from the Lord gave me fresh strength and anointing that His plans would come to pass no matter what man says. (paraphrase from Jeremiah 29).

God wants to germinate those seeds that have been planted in all of us. What we need to do is continuously praise God through those night seasons and "count it all joy" as James 1:2 states. This is one of the life lessons that I had to learn, especially as doors were closed before me through my appeal process of requesting a shorter sentence. I know this looks bleak and dark while in my valley but remember God knows what He is doing. God needed to do some works within me, hence the ten years in prison. He decided when it was time for me to file my clemency and told me when to do it. He is the one who put the lawyers in my path to take my case. The only reason all of this is occurring is because I surrendered *everything*, and I mean everything to Him - my life, my family, my past, my friendships, everything. Hollie and I have been praying for the last two years on my clemency, leaning on each other with each trial that God put me through in the clemency process. It has definitely been a long, wet with tears, two years.

Guess what, we are much closer to the end of my valley of darkness! Isn't God amazing? First Peter 1:3-9 states,

"Blessed be the God and Father of our Lord Jesus Christ!
According to his great mercy,
he has caused us to be born again to a living hope

through the resurrection of Jesus Christ from
the dead, to an inheritance that is imperishable,
undefiled, and unfading, kept in heaven
for you, who by God's power are being guarded
through faith for a salvation ready to be
revealed in the last time. In this you rejoice,
though now for a little while, if necessary,
you have been grieved by various trials,
so that the tested genuineness of your faith –
more precious than gold that perishes though it is
tested be fire - may be found to result in
praise and glory and honor at the revelation of Jesus Christ.
Though you have not seen him, you love him.
Though you do not now see him, you believe in him and
rejoice with joy that is inexpressible and filled with glory,
obtaining the outcome of your faith,
the salvation of your souls."

There are key themes in the book of First Peter that truly resound within my life and my story.

1) Those who suffer as Christians will be exalted

2) The Church of Jesus Christ is the new Temple, a new Jerusalem, the new People of God

3) Believers should set their hope on the end time inheritance

4) Christ died as a substitute for sinners (all of us), and his death is the basis for our new life

5) Christ's suffering is an example to his disciples

6) At his resurrection, Christ triumphed over his enemies

7) Christians should live righteously in their homes and in society

8) New life in Christ is the basis for a life of love and holiness.

Christians are to endure suffering for the sake of Christ, looking back on Christ's suffering and forward the consummation of salvation in his second coming. God's word has surely kept me and his assignments have transformed my life. This is what I prayed for and He answered with such power like the prophet Isaiah talks about in Isaiah 54:14-17. All this has been done, not just myself but for generations to come, for lost souls that God so loves. If God gave his only begotten son, you know how much He loves you and me.

I know the plans I have for you

I have been waiting patiently, working on myself and experiencing God's presence to change me through this wilderness experience. I knew the assignments were to shape and mold my character and transform my heart and thinking.

I have taken care of two different handicapped ladies. It was a very humbling experience so very hard dealing with them and leaving my life on hold for Christ's glory. The first lady had diabetes and ended up passing away. She was treated so badly because of her crimes. I just kept my eyes on the loving Savior and loved her so that she knew Christ loved her. The second disabled lady, that I am currently taking care of, has type 1 diabetes, sickle cell anemia, and neuropathy. On top of all that she recently found out that her kidneys are malfunctioning and has to have dialysis so many times a week. It has been amazing but very hard. I know God has a great plan, no matter what happens to this assignment. I hope and pray for miracles to help her live and not die, but no one knows the thoughts and ways of God.

While waiting to see what God has in store, He has given my mom a prophesy for me to hold on to during this current season in my life. He said, "You have spent a long time second guessing... You spent a long time in futility... You have spent a long time on what seems like a desert and you asked the Lord many times, why is this dry place so unending? And you have even come to a point of giving up hope and listened to voices that have discouraged you, not only discouraged you but have taken the life out of the call that I the Lord put upon your life. You thought I made a wrong decision that I made a wrong turn...But the Lord says nothing is too hard for me and why would you think that you can change my mind about my thoughts for you...For the Lord says I know the thoughts that I have for you and the intentions for your future and the Lord says we are right on time and right on schedule and every hardship and every dry place the Lord said I ordained and I predestined and I directed. But you say, Lord why such a hard place? Because the Lord says the season I am bringing you in is one of restoration, I will restore you to the fertile lands and you say, no Lord, not in this time of drought. As it be when the nation and nations of the world rage and the Lord says, I have not moved off my throne by what the nations do. The Lord says I am not moved by thoughts of the government. The Lord says I am GOD Almighty and I move governments. With my wishes I speak and those are lowered and I speak again and they are raised the Lord says nothing is too hard for me and why would you believe the deceiver that you had somehow made a wrong turn.

As my blessing comes closer and closer, the enemy is doing his best to distract my attention from God Almighty and His will. For example, I received information that my granddaughter has been taken into CPS custody and my daughter is in jail again. The enemy will use anything to get us to take our eyes off of the Lord, which is where our help comes from. Psalms 121 says that we are to look to the hills where our help comes from.

Do you want to know what my blessing is? Clemency. When I originally put in my request, I was denied because the board wanted ten years served. This did not include time served in county. My attorney asked that that credit be given. I cried to God on my knees, literally, for a full three days. Then, to God be the glory, I received a message on Jpay from my attorney saying that they would accept my petition but wanted a full ten years in prison.

Now according to man, I receive time off for "good time," but apparently that is not part of God's plan. His glory and will always come first. So Hollie and I sit here writing this story and continue to pray. God constantly talks through her to me. Every time He gave me a message, He always gave her the same message to tell me. He told me that I had to give my clemency up to Him. He then told Hollie the same thing to tell me. God always gives confirmation when He gives you a message. Giving things over, especially things that are important, is incredibly hard to do. That is why we are told to walk by faith and not by sight.

Having a relationship with Christ is not an easy path, but it is a fulfilling one. You may think that being awarded my clemency is impossible but remember, nothing and I mean NOTHING is impossible for the Great I Am, God Almighty. We are at the end of my valley of darkness and are entering the light. God is so AMAZING! Look at what he has done for me and know he can do even more for you.

> For I know the plans I have for you, declares the LORD,
> plans for welfare and not for evil,
> to give you a future and a hope. Jeremiah 29:11 (ESV)

A letter to my offspring...

My amazing kids are Katrina, Kristina ,Kurtus. I so dearly love them and am hoping for a second chance to be there for them and to be the mom they have never had as well as be a grandma to my grandchildren. I truly am sorry for putting my children through my selfishness and taking all my childhood trauma out on them. I will hold myself accountable for my life. This journey I have chosen is all my fault I blame only myself.

What I am going to tell you now is very humbling; however, I was awakened in the middle of the night by God and He put on my heart to talk about how special my kids really are.

My Katrina, Kristine, and Kurtus are so amazing, they deserve the best in this world. I am going to finally be able to sit and listen to their hearts, cry with them, laugh with them and just sit and let them be them. I will be able to give them good advice and be healthy enough to communicate with them as well as help make wise choices through our various difficulties. My kids deserve a changed and healthy mother and that is what I am today, a healthy person. I have worked on myself to become extraordinary and they deserve this more than I can truly explain. I hope and pray for our restoration.

God says in His word that He would restore all the years the locusts have taken from us. He says in His word, "I will restore to you the years that the swarming locust has eaten, the hopper, the destroyer, and the cutter, my great army, which I sent among you." (Joel 2:25) Did God say which He sent among us? Yes. He allowed us to go through the trials over and over, losing our material goods, friendships, family until we could get it right. God is finally going to give me this all back because of His grace and mercy first and foremost, then as well as my obedience to Him and dedication to do His will and surrendering my old behavior and being accountable for what I did wrong to my kids, grandkids, my family and the community. I hope and pray someday my children will forgive me as well as the community?

My first born, Katrina, has always been a loving, caring, funny, amazing person. She loved to cuddle up with me and tell me, "Mommy, I love you." She was one of my parent's favorite grandchildren. They spoiled her rotten! My dad always played with her and whenever my parents took her home they would always go really slow in the country so she could see the cows and horses. She absolutely loved that time with them. I love her dearly and look forward to renewing our relationship and be the mother/daughter set that God intended us to be, as well as a grandparent to her children and being able to form a relationship with them.

Kristina, my middle child, was in and out of my life because of my issues. When she was in my life, she was playful and rambunctious. Like her sister, Kristina, she loved to give hugs and cuddle. She loved to clog and still does to this day. She is absolutely phenomenal in the form of dancing that she has chosen. She is beautiful and looks as if she should be in the modeling industry. I can't wait to spend time with her and my grandkids! I am so looking forward to being a mom to her and a grandma to her four beautiful children, my grandchildren.

Kurtis, my only son, was not in my life during his infancy and the majority of his childhood. Before this sentence, I would go to the home where he was being raised, to visit and work on some form of a parent/child relationship. His adoptive mother was an angel to me. Her name is Alasca Brough. She is an amazing woman of God who raised Kurtis and Kristina in the ways of God. She took care of them, raised them during my incarcerations. God put her in my life just for the purpose of keeping my babies safe while I was working on getting my life in order, as God wanted it, surrendering my all and putting God first in everything. Now that I have arrived at the spot where God wants me to be, I will finally get the chance to be the mom that they deserve and share God's love with them, as well as be apart of the lives of Kurtis' loving children. I pray and think about them every day. There is not a moment that goes by where I don't think about them and pray for their salvation, safety, and future.

Mom loves you, Katrina, Kristina, and Kurtus and all my grandkids. I appreciate you as gifts from GOD and will be a responsible mother from here on out.

YOUR LOVING MOTHER, KIMBERLY PHILLIPS

God wants to set you free!

I am going to end my story with some food for thought. This is from "The Word For You Today" Saturday November 11, 2017: "If the Son makes you free, you shall be free indeed." John 8:36. When you become a prisoner of war, the enemy controls all your movements and decides what each day of your life will be like.

Has the enemy captured you? Perhaps you've tried over and over again to be free from your addiction but you are still imprisoned by it. There is good news: "If the Son makes you free, you shall be free indeed." Whether you are addicted to drugs, lust, alcohol, gambling, food, or anything else, your answer is not natural - but supernatural. Your addiction is a "symptom" of a deeper spiritual condition that Jesus the Great Physician wants to heal.

At the core of every twelve-step program is this truth: It's only by turning to a power greater than ourselves and developing a relationship with Him, that we can get free and stay free. And we know who that "power" is . . . Jesus!

When you feel "restless, irritable, and discontent," His presence is what brings peace and serenity.

When you're tempted to turn to your addiction to find relief, His presence fills the emptiness within you and enables you to say no.

When you experience "euphoric recall" and begin to think about the best times of your addiction rather than the worst ones, His Word renews your mind and reframes your attitude, showing you the right path to take at that moment: "By your words I can see where I'm going; they throw a beam of light on my dark path" (Psalms 119:105).

Peter said, "The Lord knows how to deliver the godly out of temptations" (2Peter 2:9). Today God wants to set you free.

[11]For I know the plans I have for you, declares the LORD, plans for welfare and not for evil, to give you a future and a hope. [12] Then you will call upon me and come and pray to me, and I will hear you.
[13] You will seek me and find me, when you seek me with all your heart. - Jeremiah 29:11-13

Made in the USA
Middletown, DE
02 April 2019